Multiple Overlapping Truths: A Mixed-Race Identity Development Workbook

Lola Osunkoya

Published by Neither Both LLC, 2023.

MULTIPLE OVERLAPPING TRUTHS: A MIXED-RACE IDENTITY DEVELOPMENT WORKBOOK

First edition. September 2, 2023.

Copyright © 2023 Lola Osunkoya.

ISBN: 979-8218271251

Written by Lola Osunkoya.

Table of Contents

Dedicated to grown up mixed kids

Navigating identity later in life

On their way to peace, belonging, and embodiment.

INTRODUCTION

———

My name is Lola Osunkoya, and I use she/her pronouns as a cishet-identifying woman. I am a Licensed Professional Clinical Counselor (LPCC) living and practicing on Dakota ancestral land, colonially known as Minneapolis, MN. I founded my private practice, Neither/Both LLC, in 2013 and previously blogged about mixed-race experiences under that same moniker.

I identify as Mixed and Black. My dad was from Nigeria, and my mom is a white woman from Minnesota of Scandinavian ancestry. My dad was deported before I was born, and I didn't meet him until I was 29 when I took a solo trip to Nigeria to meet that side of the family. I was raised in my mom's small white family, in somewhat multiracial and multicultural neighborhoods, a white Baptist church community, and the Minneapolis Public School System (primarily white, but also somewhat multiracial and multicultural). I'm from Gen X, born and raised in South Minneapolis in the 1980s and 90s. There are geographical, ethnic, historical, and social markers and programming that I grew up with here. These impact how I look at race, and your contexts influence how you look at race. All of us exist within context.

In my white family, I grew up enculturated in whiteness without anyone to talk to about my racialized experiences. My shy attempts were often met with a gentle defense of the other well-meaning white people or an explanation of Blackness and Black culture from my white mother. None of these options felt good, authentic, or affirming, so I learned to keep my questions and perceptions to myself and assumed from my child-brain that I must be misunderstanding something about race and my racialized experiences.

I

Over the years, this (along with other life experiences) contributed to the idea that I couldn't trust my perception of what was happening to me. It also led to people-pleasing and fawning behaviors to minimize the otherness I felt in my environment.

I started going to therapy as a client in my late 20s under the framing of depression. It took longer to understand and more accurately contextualize that I had some trauma and abuse in my history, much of it with an overlapping context of race. I saw therapists who addressed my clinical needs and symptoms, which was very helpful. But very few brought race into the picture in a significant, integrated way. And deep down, I knew somehow that race was inextricably intertwined with my mental and emotional health.

I live in a city with a pretty good-sized mixed population. And yet, we don't talk to each other. Clients sometimes admit that I'm the first mixed person they've ever talked to or at least the first mixed therapist they had access to.

I can only imagine how being genuinely isolated geographically and socially in mixedness would feel. But as a child and growing up, I was isolated in my mind. I didn't start talking about race until my late 20s. And my way into it was by stumbling upon research about mixed identity experiences. When I saw this research, I was dumbfounded.

Are there other people thinking this hard about race? Thinking about the same things I've been too afraid to say out loud? Having similar experiences and self-perceptions as me? You mean... I'm not oddly obsessed with race?

When I finally decided to pursue a career as a therapist, I knew race had to be fully integrated (no pun intended).

MULTIPLE OVERLAPPING TRUTHS: A MIXED-RACE IDENTITY DEVELOPMENT WORKBOOK

To be mixed is to often be without a path to follow, making your own way. I started to cobble my path by finding that research, asking more questions, and pursuing more answers through my master's thesis. I studied the research on Black/white mixed people who struggled to fit in and paired that research with the Adlerian concept of Social Interest (that belonging happens in two parts - the feeling of belonging to your community AND the act of contributing to your community). And I eventually linked up with other people working on this path in their own ways.

I don't want it to take as long for others as it took for me to begin to unpack the complexities of identity, mistaken beliefs, and internalized racism. And with my education, over a decade of providing therapy, building personal relationships, and having opportunities to be in community and create conferences through the local organization, *MidWest Mosaic (formerly known as MidWest Mixed)*, I now have more of the breadth and depth of my path paved out. This book allows me to give back and share what I've learned.

And yet, with all my personal and professional experience, I know that my knowledge and opinions may soon be outdated and undoubtedly subjective. The culture evolves quickly these days. So I have to admit that I am afraid to write this book, shy about its relevance. A young part of me that experienced many identity challenges is terrified to publish this book and subject myself to the vulnerability, scrutiny, and harshness that often surrounds conversations about mixedness. But that little girl deeply needed this book, and she needed the evolved adult woman who wrote it. So I'm practicing courage.

As a therapist today, I see about 20 clients a week and maintain a waiting list. I want to offer something tangible to people who are geographically without access to mixed communities. I hope people will work together in groups with this book, or maybe you can share what you're working on with a trusted therapist. This person might be a mixed therapist or someone with good enough skills to hold your identity carefully.

This workbook is my contribution. This is my love letter to grown-up mixed kids realizing they have some work to do.

My wish for mixed people is to claim and live identities grounded in authenticity and accuracy by:

1) practicing the courage to face complex truths,

2) learning the skills to explore history and heritage, and

3) developing language for a self-created narrative.

A Word about the Term, Mixed, and Who This Book Is for

Throughout this workbook, I will discuss language and encourage you to find the language that works for you. *Mixed* is a term I've been settled on for most of my life that works well for me; it feels accurate and authentic in my body. To some other people, *mixed* is a dirty word. Language constantly evolves, connotations change, and we all have personal preferences.

What I mean by *mixed* is sometimes specific but also expansive and inclusive.

By *mixed*, I specifically mean having two parents of distinct races/ heritages/cultures. But at the same time, I think about *mixed* in terms of a mixed experience - crossing cultures and navigating more than one set of distinct cultural rules and expectations from a young age.

And is that experience specific to people with parents of different races? Absolutely not.

MULTIPLE OVERLAPPING TRUTHS: A MIXED-RACE IDENTITY DEVELOPMENT WORKBOOK

Because of the way I have experienced my mixedness, I understand that there is a lot of identity overlap with transracial and transnational adoptees, 1.5 and second-generation children of immigrants, monoracial Black, Indigenous, and People of Color (BIPOC) who have had to navigate primarily white settings for most of their lives, people who navigate gender and sexuality spectrums, people of mixed ancestry who self-identify as monoracial but still resonate with some of these internal and navigational experiences, people of mixed heritage who are read as white but have a richly layered but invisibilized experience of race, and on and on. Additionally, I want to be clear that while many people internally default to Black and white when they think of mixed people, endless racial expressions of mixedness include neither Black nor white.

So *mixed* is both specific and a catch-all for the experience.

When I first came into a community with Midwest Mosaic, I remember someone naming that going into monoracial spaces, especially Black spaces, it felt inappropriate to center experiences as light-skinned or mixed people, but we still needed space to talk. I couldn't agree more. Racism, anti-Blackness, and colorism are all parts of this conversation. Black and monoracial voices of color need to have spaces to be centered and not derailed by obliviousness and the taking up of space by people who haven't explored their privileges. That's a thing, and many mixed people have work to do there.

But the end of that conversation isn't that mixed people just need to be quiet. Mixed people also need appropriate safe spaces to talk about their experiences, unpack privilege and oppression, and generally be seen and heard. I consistently advocate for mixed people to take up *appropriate* space. My purpose is to help create that safe space for reflection and accountability.

This book is not for everyone. And if the centering here offends you, then respectfully, it wasn't made for you. And I fully support that you deserve to find safe spaces that also center you.

Additionally, I am not for everyone. Some will resonate with my perspective, and some will not.

But if you resonate, no matter what your specific racial, ethnic, or cultural background, I'm talking to you. This book is for you.

IDENTITY EXPLORATION WITH COURAGE AND SELF-COMPASSION

You may already know the more profound beliefs guiding your perceptions about your racial identity. You may also be aware of stereotypes about yourself and others you have internalized that feel harmful. Alfred Adler said, "Kids are wonderful observers but terrible interpreters." If, from a young age, you witnessed and experienced stereotypes, misunderstandings, assumptions, and judgments about your race, your mind had to create a structure to make sense of it all. You had to find a way to safely navigate the world by predicting how others would treat you.

And I don't tiptoe around the fact that most people reading this grew up under white supremacy and many other systems of oppression. We were enculturated into it before we had words for it.

So in understanding that many of your beliefs about race began in childhood, you must treat yourself with the compassion and grace you would give a child, especially as you come up against the ugly stuff.

A child has a primarily emotional brain with minimal complex reasoning (which only fully develops in your mid-20s!). So please have compassion for your child-logic, which has informed your brain, social development, and general life expectations. Creating a new belief is vital in this process:

No matter what happened, you were never trying to do anything wrong.

You just didn't have the brain development and skills to conceptualize something as complex and full of minefields as race in our world.

As a trauma therapist, I define trauma as something beyond your ability to cope with when it happened. And trauma causes profound shifts in your perspective after it happens; it changes how you think about yourself and the world, creating mistaken beliefs. So for me and the people I work with, racialized trauma is real. On my blog, I have a post containing three short videos about trauma. It takes about 20 minutes to watch and will give you a good foundation: https://www.neitherboth.com/post/don-t-be-ashamed-of-your-trauma-response

In my training, I've learned that self-compassion is one of the most important ways to heal and reframe traumas. Self-compassion is gentleness, unconditional positive regard, grace, and a willingness to see yourself and all the factors of your life in full context. I will encourage you to use self-compassion for those mistaken beliefs you created as a child to make sense of your world, which today may seem racist, harmful, and illogical. Ultimately, I'm asking you to use self-compassion every step while exploring your identity formation, where you are today, and where you plan to expand your identity into the future.

Sometimes a triggering thought or belief will show up in your body through increased heart rate, negative thoughts, anxiety, or depression. Guided meditations and other self-soothing practices can be beneficial in calming you down and grounding you. Start practicing some of these regularly to lay the groundwork for calm. If you practice when you feel good or neutral, you can reach for these skills more easily when in a hard place. Here are a few keywords you can look up on your favorite meditation app, YouTube, or TikTok.

- Grounding or sensory grounding

- Body scan meditation

- Lovingkindness meditation

- Regulating your nervous system

- Turning on your parasympathetic nervous system

- Stimulating the vagus nerve

- Coping strategies for depression, anxiety, or trauma

Discouragement. Encouragement. Courage.

Consider the idea that you may have been deeply discouraged about your race by the questions, assumptions, and assertions of other people. Perhaps throughout childhood, you received too much pushback when you were trying to belong, and people challenged your identity one too many times. Discouragement happens when you notice a pattern of things not working out.

What happens when people continually tell you you're not who you know yourself to be? Externally, you might respond in any number of ways: shutting down ("whatever you say"), fighting back ("Yes, I am Korean - and you can catch these hands!"), or deflecting ("That's why yo mama so skinny I saw her hang gliding on a Dorito ..."). But on the inside, we may have become deeply discouraged by the expectations of others about our race, which takes energy away from grounding into and exploring ourselves.

Encouragement is an essential tool in transforming those discouraged beliefs and behavior patterns. It's about looking directly into the eyes of the discouraged part of yourself and building yourself back up again. Encouragement is grounding into your strengths and wisdom. It's a practice that starts small and helps you to build confidence step by step. It's telling the truth in the face of lies or misunderstandings other people have about you.

I know many people have had ideas about my identity, but I know how I feel inside, and there's more I want to know about myself and my heritage. I can learn what I always wanted to know.

It can be scary to decide to change, particularly to buck the system created around you by people you care about, respect, or fear. Courage is being afraid and doing it anyway.

Like self-compassion, courage is a necessary skill we must cultivate and practice in identity work. It takes courage to explore your life experiences, perceptions, and reactions. You may come up against some ugly truths in examining your life and the resulting beliefs you developed about yourself and the world. Courage is the action you take to support your growth and evolution. It's a practice.

AN IDENTITY DICTATED BY OTHERS

———

There's an interesting phenomenon with mixed people where the people around us - family, friends, community, and especially strangers - feel emboldened to give an opinion about our identities. Whether through comments, debates, social media posts, or a casual but firm statement, the message is loud and clear: *Other people have an authoritative take on my identity, and I need to consider that as I learn and decide who I am.*

And where do their hot takes come from? Their experiences, social and cultural programming, history, structural racism, colorism, white supremacy, gatekeeping, racialized fears - many places.

Mixed people have often felt judged and limited by being defined by others. We may have feelings of shame or doubt around identity because others have opinions in direct opposition to our internal and lived experiences.

A common question that most mixed people have repeatedly experienced is, "What are you?" When people can't quite fit you into a preconceived racial box, it makes them uncomfortable. They project that discomfort onto us, feeling emboldened to demand clarification through personal questions. It's bizarre. And suppose we answer in a way that challenges their perceptions or politics. In that case, this interaction can get quite uncomfortable and problematic.

And what are the impacts of a lifetime of these identity challenges for mixed folks? There are a set of shared thoughts, feelings, and behaviors that a lot of mixed people experience that can leave them with an unstable, uncomfortable sense of identity and an overall feeling of discouragement and confusion:

<u>Common Thoughts:</u>

- I'm not _____ enough

- I don't have a right to speak up/show up in spaces

- I can never show up as my whole self

- I don't belong here/anywhere

- I'm not living up to how other people expect me to be based on how I look

- I don't know how to release this discomfort/pain about my race

<u>Common Feelings:</u>

- I feel perpetually uncomfortable, like an imposter

- I feel isolated, anxious, fearful, ashamed, sad, lonely

- I feel guilty about my privilege even though I'm a POC

<u>Common Behaviors:</u>

- Becoming a chameleon

- Becoming invisible, hiding, and making myself small in public spaces

- Emphasizing other identities over my race

- Being awkward and inauthentic

The next page is the first of twelve Reflections, where I invite you to think about your personal experiences. I recommend you keep all your reflections in one place (a notebook, document, or notetaking app) because you will reference them throughout this workbook.

REFLECTION ONE:

MY THOUGHTS, FEELINGS, AND BEHAVIORS RELATED TO MY IDENTITY

Reflection and Articulation: Which of these statements resonate with your life experience? Write more if you find this list incomplete.

<u>Common Thoughts:</u>

- I'm not _____ enough

- I don't have a right to speak up/show up in spaces

- I can never show up as my whole self

- I don't belong here/anywhere

- I'm not living up to how other people expect me to be based on how I look

- I don't know how to release this discomfort/pain about my race

<u>Common Feelings:</u>

- I feel perpetually uncomfortable, like an imposter

- I feel isolated, anxious, fearful, ashamed, sad, lonely

- I feel guilty about my privilege even though I'm a POC

Common Behaviors:

- Becoming a chameleon

- Becoming invisible, hiding, and making myself small in public spaces

- Emphasizing other identities over my race

- Being awkward and inauthentic

Others:

A LITTLE ADLERIAN FRAMING

E arlier, I mentioned Social Interest, which is an Adlerian concept. Alfred Adler was a peer of Freud and created his own philosophy of psychology, including some thoughts on belonging. A central concern in identity work, especially for mixed people, is the feeling of not belonging. I liked Adler's concept of Social Interest and the framing that belonging is not only a feeling but also how you contribute to your community.

This contribution piece became real for me during my internship with *African American Family Services (AAFS)*. I was learning how to do therapy but also having an identity exploration and development experience. At AAFS, I worked primarily with Black staff, supervisors, and clients. Initially, I was nervous about being accepted and seen as authentic because of my long-term insecurities about my mixedness and Blackness. More specifically, it was about the way I talk, having been socialized in white spaces. Frankly, I thought the Black people would throw me out as soon as I opened my mouth.

Instead, I found acceptance as I showed up authentically and took risks to ask questions and share my insights. As I started to feel more accepted and valued, I also remember having the distinct thought that if I could contribute my strengths anywhere, I wanted to contribute here, to find a way to be useful here in the Black community. It was a significant corrective belonging experience.

To dig deeper into how contributing to your communities is imperative in supporting identity work, I want to introduce a few Adlerian concepts: *Basic Needs and Life Tasks, Task Orientation, Inferiority Feelings, Striving for Superiority,* and *Safeguarding.* These concepts will help normalize how many of us coped with not belonging and how we withdrew our contribution. Out of that pain of not belonging, we sometimes develop strategies that were adaptive and brilliant in childhood but don't feel so good now. Understanding how the problem was created will help you begin to identify solutions. But buckle up because this can be kind of a *read*.

Basic Needs and Life Tasks

According to Adler, we have three basic emotional needs: *Safety, Significance, and Belonging.* These needs are interconnected and vital, but we focus on *Belonging* for this book.

Additionally, we have three basic life tasks, which are the tools we use to belong in the world: *Work, Friendship, and Love/Intimacy.* For children, *work* is interchangeable with play, and *love/intimacy* can be reframed as seeing and being seen, knowing and being known.

We generally meet our needs (belonging) through participation in life tasks (play, friendship, and being seen/known) and start learning about them early.

> Example: *Nghi felt uncomfortable with how people reacted to her name's spelling and pronunciation for as long as she could remember. She felt embarrassed when people watched her mother speak in Vietnamese with confusion and laughter. She decided it was easier to make friends and belong if she only spoke in English and made jokes about her name.*

In a child's mind, this makes sense as a way to meet the need for belonging. But it's also the beginning of a behavior pattern that reinforces the white supremacist lens that treats non-white and non-English speaking people as other and inferior. It makes her feel bad about being Vietnamese and teaches her to withdraw her contribution to keeping the language and culture alive. This experience could be a root memory of internalized racism.

Task Orientation

In navigating our needs for belonging through play, showing up authentically, and contributing to the fun, we typically use one of two lenses: contributing by cooperating with others or finding our position in a hierarchy.

There is the lens that prioritizes cooperation: "I generally see myself as equal to others; we each have our strengths and challenges. So when I seek connection, I am focused on finding common ground and bringing my strengths and goodwill to the relationship."

> Example: *Sammy sees Marcus and Jerome building a castle in the sandbox. Sammy has a shovel and approaches, smiling. He says he likes their castle and asks if he can help them dig the hole for the moat.*

And there is the lens that prioritizes your positioning in a hierarchy: "I tend to compare myself to others to see if I'm doing better or worse at fitting in or making friends. I judge myself and others rather than bringing my strengths to the connection. Contributing my gifts becomes secondary to assessing whether I am doing this right. I regularly ask, 'Am I better or worse than other people? Do they like me or not?' I've all but forgotten about what I have to contribute."

> Example: *Sammy sees Marcus and Jerome playing and laughing in the sandbox. Jerome already has the castle mold, and Marcus is digging by hand. Sammy thinks, "They don't need me and my dumb shovel. They're already friends; they probably don't want me here. I'll just go play by myself."*

All humans navigate the life task of belonging. It begins in our earliest years as we learn how to approach others. Some of us have parents who conditioned us to come from a cooperative stance, and some parents taught us to come from a comparative or competitive perspective. In a racialized society, the approach has layers - some that we bring to the table as our individual personalities and family socialization, and other layers are more systemic and out of our control. Subconscious programming about racial hierarchies can influence our beliefs about belonging, but we can learn to be more cooperative.

Inferiority Feelings

Inferiority feelings are, in some ways, a natural part of being human. We all experience the helplessness of navigating the world as dependent children who can't do everything for themselves. We depend on parents and other adults to help us fulfill our physical, emotional, and social needs. Early on, we can feel lost without their guidance. Navigating race as part of our social need for belonging can be incredibly complex; if we feel like we're not doing it right, this can lead to a special kind of inferiority feeling.

Our early caregivers can have a significant impact on how we experience inferiority. Some caregivers help us learn to adapt and take risks to figure out how to make friends. Other caregivers, consciously or not, may discourage our independence and confidence by passing down their beliefs and insecurities or doing things for us that we could learn to do for ourselves. And again, this can have racialized layers involving different cultural norms around connection. While many people have been trained to find ways to belong to family, community, and society, some get discouraged by these inferiority feelings.

Example: *Jinessa, a Black/white biracial girl who lives with her white dad and his family, enjoys playing jump rope at home alone, but she's too scared to ask to try double dutch with the little Black girls on the playground. She wants to be friends and try something she might be good at, but they have been teasing her about her dialect, so Jinessa believes she will never fit in with them. Her dad dismisses her concern and says she talks just fine and to keep asking.*

Jinessa's dad's ignorance could intensify her sense of inferiority and shyness around Black peers by not validating her concerns and the differences in language use and dialect that impact connection.

Striving for Superiority

When people feel insecure because they don't belong, it's normal to compensate by trying to be better than somebody else. Striving for superiority can go in a positive or negative direction.

When someone strives positively, they use that lens that prioritizes cooperation - they use their strengths and skills to contribute to the community. Negative striving is the lens that compares yourself to others and tries to find a way to be on top.

E.D Ferguson wrote in 2010 about Adler's ideas about belonging. "Once the child feels that they do not belong, behaviors are then directed toward self-protection rather than a contribution to the community... Children who do not feel belonging strive to be special rather than strive to contribute." This self-protection tactic can also take the form of masking or perfectionism.

Example: *Miguel has always been good at basketball but has had trouble fitting in socially. While the coaches and his dad tell him to be a team player, he projects his social inferiority on the court by showing off and hogging the ball. It makes him feel better, somehow vindicated in being better than the other kids.*

He works hard to perfect his skills but struggles to make friends with his teammates and perceives that they're all jealous of him as the star shooter.

Safeguarding

When mixed people have experiences similar to the ways described above, wounds can develop around belonging. There can be repeated social experiences that reinforce the idea, "Something is wrong with me; I don't belong." It can feel like a blurry-edged sense of defectiveness or unlovability, which can feel shameful. And the thing about shame is that most people would prefer to cover it up than address and heal it.

And sometimes, there are legitimate reasons for not wanting to belong. The wounds can be so deep and painful, and the rejection so pointed that it causes a discouragement so deep that you give up.

Or perhaps "cultural norms" became equated with negative stereotypes we don't relate to or align with. I first heard about *stereotype vulnerability* through K.A. Renn's research (2008), and a lightbulb went off, providing a name for what I observed growing up in Minneapolis.

When ethnic communities are small and embedded within spheres of whiteness, the rules of belonging can become rigid. Being marginalized from whiteness provokes, in some communities, the need for self-protection and clear differentiation. Sometimes the norms can be strictly gatekept by the smaller communities, and the differences may become a sense of pride. However, this can backfire.

Consider how some marginalized communities will attack their own for "acting white" by doing well in school. "If this is how I have to act to be accepted by this group of Black people... I don't want it." Diverse intracultural representation matters - lived experiences can be differently validated in larger, more diverse communities that more accurately represent all Blackness can be.

When someone feels something intangibly wrong with them, the brain can work overtime to hide and protect that pain. The purpose of *safeguarding* is to deflect attention from a person's areas of perceived weakness. So instead of accepting and working on their inexperience, inabilities, and insecurities, people can create a type of sideshow to give possible reasons for not participating in the work it takes to find community. People find ways to compensate for feeling left out, and we call this safeguarding.

Carlson, Watts, & Maniacci (2005) present several different categories of safeguarding:

<u>Symptoms</u> are unconscious fears, real or imagined physiological complaints, and obsessive thoughts or behaviors.

> Example: *Maria, a Colombian adoptee within a white family, developed laryngitis before the play so she didn't have to speak Spanish in front of the whole school and get teased about her American accent.*

<u>Excuses</u> are ways one consciously rationalizes or denies thoughts and behaviors to avoid unwanted tasks.

> *Example: Elizabeth, Liberian and Italian, had given up trying to make friends with the other Liberian kids at church, even though her father kept pressing her to be more friendly. Her private logic said, "Liberian people always reject me anyway, so I just don't need to try anymore." Underneath this narrative is the fear of being rejected again.*

<u>Aggression</u> is expressed through the subcategories of:

21

• *Depreciation* (putting others down to feel better about oneself)

○ Example: *Octavia, Black and Filipina, has felt left out in traditional Filipino circles but has tried to gain status by putting down the Filipino and white kids with lighter skin and less pronounced features.*

• *Accusation* (deflecting blame outside of oneself for their problems or failures),

○ Example: *Even as a middle-aged person, Jack blames his Iranian father for not teaching him language and culture, and to this day blames his father for not being able to fit in anywhere.*

Distance-Seeking is a way to avoid significant tasks by:

• *Backward Movement* (a well-timed failure),

○ Example: *Jose, Dakota and Mexican, didn't grow up on the res with his dad's family and feels uncomfortable because there are parts of the culture he doesn't understand. He was invited to stay with his auntie and cousins for a week and was scared but looking forward to seeing what it was like. At the last minute, he canceled, saying he was sick, and went to the cabin with a white friend instead because he couldn't face the fear of judgment and rejection.*

• *Standing still* (consistently stopping before task completion),

○ Example: *Charlotte, whose parents are from Namibia and Australia, is a visual artist who has shown various works and seen a lot of success. She wants to create work from her last trip to Namibia, and she has started many canvases but continues to put the unfinished work in a trunk in storage, afraid of the public reaction to claiming this part of her identity.*

- *Hesitation* (back-and-forth movement without full task completion),

○ Example: *Part of Maryam is excited about going to the Hindu temple with a new friend but she is afraid of not being seen as Indian enough. So she keeps texting Fatima to say hi but backs out whenever they make plans.*

- *Creating obstacles* (making an unreachable goal a roadblock to full task completion);

○ Example: *Even though he has had the money saved for years, Mukasa has set a rigid boundary around readiness to make a first trip to Uganda. "I have to research everything and be fluent in Swahili before I travel to my birth country."*

Anxiety is used when a person tries to avoid failure by being too afraid to face a task.

Example: *Chue wants the papaya salad he used to eat with his family in Fresno. But his Hmong is so limited since he moved away as a kid he's afraid to go in and order.*

Exclusion Tendency is a mechanism where people participate only in tasks in which success is guaranteed, and all other tasks are avoided.

Example: *Mariella, Black and Puerto Rican, lived most of her life in Watts. Recently her family moved back to her dad's hometown in the Humboldt Park neighborhood of Chicago. The Spanish she learned in junior high differs from how her Puerto*

Rican classmates speak, so she just tells everyone she's Black, aligns herself with the Black kids, and refuses to speak anything but English. It upsets her dad, but she can't handle the social rejection.

Feeling like you don't belong hurts, and it's human to want to hide what makes you feel vulnerable. You're in good company if you recognize yourself in some of these safeguarding techniques. Remember, you were never trying to do anything wrong on purpose.

However, if you're going to move forward and think about yourself in a new way, it's essential to be honest with yourself about the tactics you've used to avoid rejection. It may have kept you safe, but it also kept you apart, and we're looking for ways to come together. The following reflection is an opportunity for you to clarify how you have compensated for feeling like you couldn't fit in.

REFLECTION TWO:

MY INFERIORITY FEELINGS AND COMPENSATIONS

What are my inferiorities around my racial identity?

How did I find my belonging?

How have I oriented to the task of racial belonging or fitting in?

What are my patterns around striving?

Which of the safeguarding self-preservation strategies have I used?

Summary

At this point, you have identified some of your more limiting thoughts, feelings, and behaviors related to mixedness. You've looked at how children learn to belong by navigating the tasks of friendship and play. You've learned how children develop a cooperative way of participating with others or a hierarchical form of determining worth through comparison. And you have reflected on some of the more dysfunctional ways you might be compensating for feeling left out. We've got some of the more challenging pieces out on the table. My guess is you don't want to continue with these beliefs and defenses for the rest of your life.

The good news is that when we know what we don't want, we know what we do want (hot tip - they're opposites). I'm inviting you to find a way to transform these narratives, which were created in reaction to external judgment that became internalized. I'm asking you to find a way to create an identity narrative that works for you.

Many mixed people struggle with being privileged or oppressed or both. I invite you to consider a path of dignity and humility as you integrate your privilege and oppression. We are not a set of dichotomies. We live with multiple overlapping truths. These truths are complex and confusing sometimes, but rather than chasing either/or, we could acknowledge that we're *all* of it.

As I mentioned, our brains develop until age 25, and our childhood experiences impact our brain and social development. I am curious about the impact of navigating complexity from such a young age, even before we have the cognitive wiring or language to make sense of it.

Holding the outward expectations about who we are and how we should see ourselves, early training to respond differently based on the setting, the people, or the language involved, learning to be a chameleon as a survival mechanism... How does this contribute to our capacity for mental flexibility, problem-solving, and mental and social creativity? Certainly, there are plenty of challenges to being mixed. But what about the gifts?

Consider that another common experience we share as mixed people is a deep capacity for complexity and overlap. Lean into the multiple overlapping truths. They are our superpowers!

And so, with your superpower in hand, I want to share with you some of the ways researchers have thought about how identity develops, evolves, and expands.

There are a variety of identity development models available to assist you in exploring how your identity has developed. *Stages of Development* models talk about how identity develops over the lifetime; *Social Context* models look at various contexts within which identity develops. Both can be useful in their own ways because identity can change over time and between contexts.

STAGES OF DEVELOPMENT MODELS

———

M any researchers have studied identity by focusing on a series of stages. These stages help articulate how people move from an unconscious alignment with white supremacy to self-definition and embodiment.

In the 1960s, William Cross became interested in understanding Black people's language and identity transformation in America. His *'Negro to Black' Conversion Experience* focused on why specific activating experiences would force an examination of racism and personal racial identity. He identified these stages:

Pre-Encounter: Unawareness of race and its social implications, but identifying with white people and culture, devaluing Black people and culture.

Encounter: An experience that suddenly brings the fact that we are racialized beings within a white supremacist society, forcing us to come to terms with our own racial identity.

Immersion/Emersion: The active choice to immerse oneself in Black culture and prove Blackness while divesting from and rejecting whiteness (typically emotionally and defensively driven).

Internalization: Beginning to resolve the internal identity conflicts, internalizing a sense of Black identity without needing to prove anything, and often ready to connect meaningfully with people of other races.

Internalization/Commitment: An increasing level of comfort in Blackness and the racial identity of others, resisting forms of social oppression, and participating in social activism.

I chose Cross's as the only illustration of stage models because his was the earliest. Many thinkers have adapted, added, and increased the complexity of these stages over time for many ethnicities, genders, sexualities, and other identity experiences. I have examples here: https://www.neitherboth.com/post/identity-development-models

Below, I've taken some liberties and broadened the definitions of the stages to make them more general, and offered some sample thoughts and experiences:

Pre-Encounter: Before becoming aware of race and its social implications, embeddedness in white normativity and white supremacy that saturates our laws, systems, media, and social/cultural training.

- Raised in a white family or within a white community and learning to assimilate into white social norms

- Preferring white dolls and stories featuring white characters, buying into social and media programming that devalues BIPOC without any kind of critical analysis

Encounter/Activating Event: An experience that suddenly clarifies our racialization within a white supremacist society, forcing us to come to terms with racial identity and its implications.

- Experiencing a racial slur for the first time

- Noticing that social programming that works for white people doesn't work for you

- Witnessing racism individually, within your family or community, or in social structures

Immersion/Emersion: Typically emotionally and defensively driven, the active choice to immerse oneself in non-white cultural backgrounds and prove loyalty to those cultural identities while divesting from and rejecting whiteness.

- "No new white people"

- Deciding to only be around BIPOC or more specific intersectional communities

- Pulling away from white family or friends while beginning to notice the ways they are unaware of how white supremacy has impacted their lives, beliefs, and behaviors

Internalization: Beginning to resolve the internal identity conflicts, internalizing a sense of your cultural and ethnic identity without needing to prove anything, and often ready to connect meaningfully with people of other races.

- Feeling more comfortable with your chosen identities

- Feeling more confident using your preferred language

- Beginning to reintegrate nuance and seeing white people as individuals who have and have not done their work

Internalization/Commitment: An increasing level of comfort in your own ethnic and cultural identities as well as the racial and cultural identities of others, resisting forms of social oppression, and participating in social activism.

- Joining BIPOC cultural affinity groups

- Supporting others in their racial identity journeys

- Becoming more active in racial and social justice circles

These stages of development are a loose map for understanding identity. Some people navigate these stages differently, and activating events can cause us to engage with the process multiple times.

And now, if we want to develop our identities further, can we give ourselves activating experiences and move forward purposefully?

A Word on Activating Experiences:

Activating events force us to rethink our racial identities and how the world generally operates (the "Encounter" stage). Reorganizing our beliefs can be complex and challenging.

We experienced a worldwide activating event with the murder of George Floyd in May 2020. Two months into the pandemic and stay-at-home orders with so much time on our hands, we witnessed and reacted to his murder within the context of race, power, corruption, and lies.

And my guess is that you, like me, like everyone watching, deeply experienced their race in a crystalizing way. Many white people suddenly understood their whiteness. Temporarily. But that's another phenomenon for another book.

For all who were willing to honestly examine what the murder of George Floyd triggered in our collective consciousness, we had a massive opportunity for identity development. With courage and humility, many took this opportunity to do genuinely transformational work.

For some of us, this was not optional work. We were very quickly swept up into the uprising and will never see ourselves and each other in the same way again. In this heightened time, as I observed clients and community, I considered a few direct questions people were asking to assess their own (and sometimes one another's) character.

Which side of the white supremacist systems and structures will you stand on?

Will you acknowledge the ways you have benefitted from white supremacy?

Are you willing to be accountable for your personal and community role in anti-Blackness?

These deeply challenging questions form an authentic and courageous exploration of identity, power, privilege, racism, and oppression.

REFLECTION THREE:

STAGES OF DEVELOPMENT

Write or draw a description of your experiences navigating the stages of development in your life. It's ok if there are stages you haven't completed or your life hasn't followed this order. Remember, this is A tool, not THE tool.

How did the murder of George Floyd (or another activating event) impact your life and your sense of identity?

What did you notice about the impacts on people of different races in your life?

Did you lose relationships?

Did you feel pressured to minimize your identities to keep peace in relationships? Is this a habit?

What other ways did you use to navigate the exposed tension of a nation clumsily trying to reckon with race?

Some people became aware of uncomfortable habits in their relationship with whiteness and white people. For example, patterns of avoiding talking about race or their own racialized experiences with white people, appeasing well-meaning white people to avoid conflict when they said things that upset you or felt subtly racist, etc. Did you become aware of any habits of concession or adjustment? During the aftermath of this activating event, did the way you habitually adjusted to whiteness suddenly feel like too much to bear?

In what other ways did this activating event impact you and your relationships?

CONTEXTUAL MODELS OF IDENTITY

═══

I prefer social context models of identity development that focus more on the contexts within which our identities develop. I have relied heavily on the work of Charmaigne Wijeyesinghe's *Factor Model of Multiracial Identity*. When I met her recently, she told me she no longer does identity work without an intersectional lens. I hope the following framing will be inclusive enough to honor the spirit of her work.

How do we understand our identities within context? Here are the categories I use (we'll dive more deeply into each context in the next reflection):

Racial Ancestry: Who are your people?

Social and Historical Context: How do history and social issues impact you and your people?

Physical Appearance: How do you look, and what does that mean - to you and others?

Early Experiences and Socialization: What did you learn about your childhood identity?

Spirituality: Do your beliefs impact your identity?

Socio-Economic Status: How do class and privilege impact how you identify?

School experiences: What did academics and peers at school teach you about race?

Gender Norms: What were the gendered expectations about your race?

Relationship Norms: What kind of relationships could you expect?

Cultural Attachment: Who did you bond with or run from?

Political Awareness and Orientation: How has your identity been politicized?

Other Social Identities: Which of your other identities are essential to who you are?

Racialized Memories As Snapshots in Time

Memories are tricky but can provide tremendous insight into how we learned to navigate the world from a young age. At Adler Graduate School, I learned that early memories provide insight into what we learned about who we are, how the world works, gender roles, racialized perceptions, and who we must be to be safe, significant, and belong.

I like using an early memory as we explore contexts because we tend to judge ourselves for the meaning we made as children. Applying the context to a particular time in life can be helpful.

My earliest racialized memory happened around age 6 or 7.

> *I went to my friend Trina's house; she was part of my Black second family. We went outside to play with some girls from the neighborhood, and I was nervous and excited to make friends. But when I opened my mouth to speak, their faces changed. "Why you talk like that? She actin' white. You think you better than us? She think she cute." I was shocked because I didn't know what I was doing wrong. Trina said, "Leave her alone. She can't help it - her mom's white!" And that was poignant for*

*me because it explained something. "So that's what's wrong with
me," I thought.*

At age 6 or 7, I learned that the way I talked was not Black, making me
seem like I was trying to be white. I learned that being cute and talking
like this meant I must think I was better than the little Black girls.

I learned that the world would perceive me as incongruent and offensive.

I learned that I wasn't doing Blackness right and that little Black girls
especially didn't like me.

At 6 or 7, I learned I should keep my mouth shut and downplay how I
looked if I wanted any chance of safety or belonging. I understood there
was something significant about how I looked and talked, but it wasn't a
good thing in every community.

My child-brain had an experience, and I made as much sense of it as
possible when it happened, but it overwhelmed me. This experience
wasn't the first time people were surprised by how I looked and talked.
But it was the first time someone clearly articulated it and gave a concrete
reason for what was so wrong with me. Even though I felt far from
superior and knew this framing didn't fit how I felt inside, I quietly
carried their assessment with me for years, assuming all Black people
secretly saw me this way and hated me.

But what about the context of that memory? Here's what my world
looked like at 6 or 7 years old:

Racial Ancestry: I came from a White American mother (who raised me)
and a Nigerian father (who the government deported before I was born).

Social and Historical Context: In the 1970s and 80s, Nigeria was
experiencing a lot of political instability. Getting out of Nigeria was (and
remains) complex, and the US had a pretty heartless immigration policy.

After my father was deported, it was near impossible for my parents to find an option to live together in either of their countries. This context contributes to why my Black parent wasn't present to physically, socially, and emotionally enculturate me into Nigerian or Black culture.

Physical Appearance: I had medium to light skin and kinky hair. In white communities, I was getting a lot of comments on how cute I was and how pretty my skin was. In Black communities, people joked disappointedly that I didn't get any of my mom's hair. Still, I felt cute because that's the feedback I primarily got back then. It was jarring to have that flipped as an accusation.

Early Experiences and Socialization: I was raised by a single white woman, socialized with a white family, schools, and church community, and lived in a multicultural neighborhood. I noticed contextual differences at a young age. My family generally referred to me as Black. In the broader community, white people gave me the idea that I was cute and special. In my neighborhood, I was just one of the kids. I was already getting special attention at school for being unexpectedly intelligent and well-spoken (we'll get to that). Overall I was getting the idea that I was different but cute and special. I had experienced confusion, questions, and curiosity as a response to my difference, but not yet anger or rejection.

Spirituality: I spent about half time with my white grandparents and their white Baptist church community. "Jesus loves the little children, All the children of the world..." I was well-loved by everyone there. So in the context of my memory, I walked in expecting to be liked, and the little Black girls' reaction crushed and confused me. I had wanted to belong to them, too.

Socio-Economic Status: I knew we were poor in my household with my mom and our neighborhood. Going to visit my grandparents and aunt and uncle, I had access to working-class or middle-class spaces - I saw how the other half lived, and those spaces were predominantly white. Minnesota has one of the broadest racial disparity gaps in the country. When I visited Trina on the northside, I knew that this was where the Black people lived and that the area was as poor and more dangerous than where we lived. I noticed different levels of poverty and how they correlated with race before I had the language for it.

School Experiences: The only thing school taught me about Africa was from National Geographic films with jungle scenes of primitive life. Black history centered exclusively on Martin Luther King, Jr. By this time, I had been singled out and enrolled in gifted and talented enrichment classes. I didn't learn until later in life about the racism of lowered expectations and the ways that white teachers and administrators exceptionalized me. At the time, I took it as a compliment and found my superiority by doing well in school. But this also separated me further from my Black peers.

Gender Norms: Because of all the special attention, I knew from a young age that my skin made me a pretty Black girl. I was lighter than many of my Black peers, and there was something about how I looked that was both valuable and hated by them. "She think she cute" was something I perceived as an accusation. And I DID think I was cute. But with those comments, I realized something was wrong with that, and I better keep it to myself around Black kids. I was conversely aware that my cuteness didn't appear to threaten white kids.

Relationship Norms: Most families in my neighborhood and my mom's friend group were single-mother homes. As a young kid, it appeared that only white families had a mom and a dad.

Cultural Attachment: My Nigerian dad was deported before I was born; periodic phone calls did not pass culture down. There were popular commercials on TV to feed the starving children in Africa, who the media depicted as malnourished and swarmed by flies. I could not access much positive information about my dad's country or culture, so I was ashamed. White people accepted me as an individual with no race, and the Black American kids challenged me for not performing Blackness as expected. My mom kept a multicultural social circle, code-switched, and tried to tell me about race and racism. Though I didn't have the words, even at a young age, something felt off about a white woman filtering blackness to me through her white experiences. My environment and my safeguarding compensations planted the seeds for anti-Blackness early.

Political Awareness and Orientation: This was not something I was aware of as a child; it became much more prevalent as an adult. Still, I was perceiving something about being cute, the way I talked, and who was better than who that hinted at the political nature of claiming identity. Many people referred to me as Black, and some asked, "What are you?" But it was evident at a young age that how I answered the question of identity was important and held weight.

Other Social Identities: I was a latch-key kid (pretty standard for my generation), leading to a lot of independent, unsupervised time alone and with friends. Being in gifted and talented classes, I was often taken out of my regular classes throughout elementary school to do special projects. Those spaces were primarily white, further isolating me from Black peers but boosting my self-esteem as a bright and creative kid. As I said, this is where I found my striving for superiority.

I had many childhood experiences, but this is among my few vivid childhood memories. At my young age and within those contexts, that experience explained something to my little girl brain.

I often felt shame about not being Black enough and the compensations I made to hide that shame. Because of these early rejections, I began building walls around Black people so I wouldn't get hurt that way anymore. As a kid, I gravitated toward non-Black peers to feel safer while continuing to hide parts of myself; no matter which circle I fled to, some part of me would be unacceptable.

And I leaned further into my intelligence and creativity to feel superior and accepted. But it was lonely because I could never fully be myself. As I grew up, I intellectually knew that Black people didn't hate me, but I couldn't shake the emotional trauma of this and other racialized rejection. It was racialized trauma, but in my heart, it felt like deep shame.

As an adult, I had to work through a lot of my anti-Blackness and process the shame that comes with it. Seeing myself in context was necessary to overcome that shame, so I could finally internalize that I was not responsible for my contexts. I had to develop more compassion for the little child, a wonderful observer but terrible interpreter. She did her best to find her safety, significance, and belonging.

I love that little girl.

And I lovingly correct her mistaken beliefs. I had no control over her contexts, but I am responsible for my growth and corrections as an adult.

Our early memories are crucial; they reveal so much about what shaped our worldviews and identities. We can look at our contexts at any age to discover what influenced our beliefs and decisions. And in comparing one time of life to another, we can learn what changed in each of our contexts to push us forward.

I also want to take a moment to normalize here that many people don't have a lot of memory for various reasons, including trauma and the brain protecting us from overwhelming experiences. So if you don't have something to work with here, that's ok too. You might still have valuable information about your contexts.

We'll now take the opportunity to look at one of your racialized memories. You'll think about why that memory was significant in making sense of your identity. Then we'll put you in context to develop compassion around your childhood decisions about race.

REFLECTION FOUR:

MEMORY AND CONTEXTS

Describe an early memory of when you were made aware of your race, racism, or racial difference.

Reflect on what meaning you have taken about race from this time. As a reminder, you might ask yourself, "What did this teach me about...?"

- Who I am

- How the world works/rules I learned about how to navigate the world

- Gender roles/racialized gender roles

- Who I have to be in order to be safe, to be significant, and to belong

- Anything else relevant to race

Now we'll take a moment to focus on the context for the version of you in this memory. Who were you at the time that this happened?. Under each category are helpful questions to support your inquiry.

My name (and feel free to use a nickname people called you around that age):

My age:

My Racial Ancestry:

- What is your birth parents' ethnic background?

- Did you grow up with them?

- Were there siblings, cousins, or other families who had the same specific racial ancestry?

- How has this impacted the concept of your own identity?

My Social and Historical Context:

- Think about your parents' (or significant caregivers') racial backgrounds. Are there any current issues or historical factors that put their ethnicities or nationalities on conflicting sides of a vital stance or piece of history? Examples: Police brutality, war, racism, immigration, feminism, slavery, internment camps, etc.

- How does that impact you to have your ancestors on opposite sides of history or current events?

My Physical Appearance:

- Describe your skin color and tone, hair color and texture, eye color and shape, size and shape of your facial features, and body structure.

- Does your look align you more with one race or the other, or do you present ambiguously?

- Do you alter your physical appearance to align yourself with one race or the other?

● Are you aware of differences in how you see yourself versus how others see you? Are you "read" differently than you perceive yourself? Which perception is more important?

My Early Experiences and Socialization:

● Describe the ethnic and cultural traditions you participated in as a child (food, music, celebration of various holidays, use of multiple languages or dialects).

● Were you instructed by parents, family, or other social communities to self-identify one way or another?

● Were there any communities you felt particularly accepted or rejected by?

My Spirituality:

● In a broad sense, do you believe in, seek meaning from, or feel guided by a sense of spirituality or a higher power?

● Does your spirituality influence the way you identify?

● Does spirituality serve as comfort or help you cope with challenges to your racial identity?

My Socio-Economic Status (SES), Class, and Privilege:

● Did your family struggle with money, have plenty, or something in between?

● Were there other families that looked like yours in your same financial situation?

• Did you interact with other people of other statuses, and how did you feel about that? Was there a racial difference associated with the difference in income?

My School Experiences:

• In terms of grades and school success, how did you do in school?

• What was school like socially for you? Who did you feel accepted or rejected by?

• Were there expectations about people of your racial background(s)? Did you meet those expectations? If not, how did that feel?

My Gender Norms:

• What sex were you assigned at birth? Did you agree with this assignment when you were old enough to self-reflect?

• How were girls of your race supposed to act and relate?

• How were boys of your race supposed to act and relate?

• Did you meet the expectations of your gender and racialized gender? If not, how did you feel and compensate?

My Relationship Norms:

• What relationship structures did you observe in childhood? (i.e., monogamy, open relationships, polyamory? Married/partnered or single parents? Parenting together or apart? Parents having partners, dating, casually dating, remarried?

Nuclear family units or extended family or community involvement?)

● From the lens of race, did you develop any expectations about who did or didn't partner or parent in your household or community?

My Cultural Attachment:

● Do you have friends of the same racial makeup and who identify the same way?

● Are there certain racial groups you are more or less comfortable with?

My Political and Social Awareness:

● Have current politics or social movements impacted your public identity?

● Are there nuances and consequences to how you do or don't publicly claim your identity?

My Other Important Identities:

● What are your other prominent identities, such as ability or disability status, age group/generation, etc?

● In what ways do your identities intersect? How do the intersections impact how you racially identify?

And considering all this context, read over your memory once more with as much compassion, curiosity, and grace as I hope you have started to develop through this exercise.

Is there anything you'd like to change about your self-perception in this memory?

THE EFFECTS OF SYSTEMS OF OPPRESSION

It's essential to acknowledge how various systems of oppression influence your identity.

Your identities do not operate in a vacuum; they are context-influenced and intersecting. Racial identity is not the only thing you're contending with; it operates alongside and intermingles with other marginalized life experiences. In the United States today, we are operating under a variety of structures of oppression, specifically:

- White Supremacy and White Normativity

- Heteronormativity and Heterosexism

- Patriarchy and Sexism

- Cis-normativity and Transphobia

- Ableism

- Other systems relevant to you (Education, Professionalism, Religion, etc.)

Your racial identity overlaps with all of these systems. Until we step out from underneath these structures of oppression, they are like the air we breathe - invisible, unquestioned, impacting how we think about ourselves and navigate the world. Operating from an intersectional identity perspective, how does your race impact and overlap your experiences of gender, sexuality, SES, etc.?

Additionally, we contend with recognized hierarchies within and among these systems of oppression - colorism, racial hierarchies, power and privilege, stereotypes, etc. Even within a system of oppression, we may have certain unearned privileges based on our social contexts and phenotypes (what we look like/our genetic expression).

At the first Midwest Mosaic Conference, our keynote speaker was Ricardo Levins Morales. He led an exercise I will never forget. He asked us to call out the structures of oppression we were operating under: "What's in the room?" We identified everything above and many more. After we named each ism, we spoke these words together as a group:

"_____ is in the room. We acknowledge you, but we do not submit to you."

Powerful.

And when I can reach for it, this is how I run my life. This is how I center the *isms* in identity work. I won't debate their existence; these things are real. But in acknowledging them, can we find a way to step out from underneath them and stand a little taller in our humanity? I choose to look at myself through a lens of liberation and dignity. This practice requires self-compassion and courage.

In addition to how these systems might oppress us, responsible identity work also requires clarity on how you benefit from these systems.

Xia (Black, Chinese, and white) may not be white or ever pass as white but benefits from white supremacy and white normativity. They grew up with both parents and a set of white grandparents in a predominantly white suburb outside of a big city. Standard white American dialect, socialization, and culture are natural to them, and they expertly navigate white spaces. Xia's voice is "professional," and they have a pretty brown face, which makes them an excellent choice for forward-facing receptionist and customer service positions. Their white socialization allowed them access to higher-income positions when they took a few years off before beginning a career in law.

Xia also identifies as able-bodied, pansexual, nonbinary, and grew up Christian. They have observed that this mix of privileges and marginalizations, visible and invisible, can impact how people treat them in different environments.

In terms of mental health, they struggle with depression, anxiety, and confidence. Many of their challenges connect to their race, gender, and sexuality - how others perceived them and challenged their sense of reality and self-knowledge. They feel the impacts of structural racism, colorism, transphobia, and homophobia.

As an AFAB (assigned female at birth) nonbinary person who tends to present as more feminine, Xia doesn't perceive themself to benefit from male privilege. Still, they have more privileges than many women due to their education, profession, and meeting traditional standards of beauty. However, they also experience this as community-dependent, receiving more pretty privilege in Black communities than in Chinese or white. Having a Chinese name with darker skin and a more ambiguous look has created a lot of internal and external conflict in Xia's life.

Systems of oppression impact us in various ways and can change based on our enculturation and community embeddedness. We can be privileged in many ways while still experiencing the damaging effects of oppression and marginalization.

REFLECTION FIVE:

THE SYSTEMS THAT IMPACTED ME

Consider the following systems and any others that significantly impact you. How do these show up in the way you navigate your racial and ethnic identities, as well as your other essential identities? Feel free to add or skip any according to your personal experience.

- White Supremacy and White Normativity

- Heteronormativity and Heterosexism

- Patriarchy and Sexism

- Cis-normativity and Transphobia

- Ableism

- Other Systems Relevant to You (Education, Professionalism, Religion, etc. Be creative)

INTEGRATING MY LIFE: BRINGING IT ALL TOGETHER WITH SELF-COMPASSION

———

At this point, we've looked at many things to bring some spaciousness and context to those young, small, rigid beliefs about your identity. We have looked at:

- Thoughts, feelings, actions, and beliefs that are common to mixed-race experiences

- Compensations we make when we feel we can't belong

- Identity development as seen through stages and activating experiences

- The many contexts in which identity develops

- Racialized memories

- The impacts of systems of oppression

If I'm looking at a person, mixed-race or not, having this much context gives me a better opportunity to see them clearly. I can better understand what contributes to their decision-making, strengths and resources, fears and challenges, and why they see themselves the way they do. I see them as individuals shaped by their access, environment, people, and experiences - you know, as a whole person. I want you to look at yourself as a whole person. And when you do that, you'll be more curious, compassionate, and open to others.

You had some experience in Reflection Four, talking about your contexts early on in identity development, and in Reflection Five, diving into how systems of oppression have shaped your child-logic. Take a moment to review those, and then think about yourself today to see how contexts have changed to bring you to your current vantage point. Maybe you're ready to tell a new story about yourself.

So how can you pull all of these together? Let's look at Javier's story.

> *Javier, a Honduran adoptee, left his small town in Ohio to attend college in California. While he met various people from different Latin American countries, he had trouble connecting and felt like he didn't belong, like he was too white. With the cultural and sometimes language barriers, Javier fell back into familiar socializing patterns with primarily white people. He came out as gay in his sophomore year. Still surrounded by whiteness because of comfort, Javier leaned more into his gay identity than his racial identity. It felt good to find community, even if he felt a little different and outside of the white standards of gay attractiveness and masculinity. Sometimes when Javier got quiet enough, he still felt the pain of not belonging and blamed himself for not trying harder. He was depressed and anxious as his friends were hooking up regularly and finding relationships. He leaned further into humor and making jokes but felt profoundly lonely and different from other Latinos. As he used these tools to explore identity, he learned and accepted more about his life experiences so far.*

Javier's Common Thoughts:

- I'm not Honduran enough; I'm not an authentic Latino

- I don't belong anywhere

- I'm not living up to what others expect. I look Latino but don't act like it.

- I don't know how to release this pain about my race.

Javier's Common Feelings:

- I have imposter's syndrome

- I feel isolated, anxious, ashamed, lonely

Javier's Common Behaviors:

- I feel more comfortable as a gay man than in claiming my Honduran heritage

- I'm awkward and inauthentic

Stages of Development and Activating Experiences: In Ohio, Javier didn't think much about his ethnicity; it was more in college and living in California that he had activating experiences around race - Latinos speaking to him in Spanish made him way more uncomfortable than white people assuming he did. The look of pity and disappointment, especially from older women, stuck with him and made him think more deeply about identity. In terms of stages of identity development, he placed himself in the *Encounter* stage.

Javier's Contexts:

Racial Ancestry: Honduran, adopted

Social and Historical Context: Honduras and the US have had a relatively amicable political and historical relationship, but there is marked financial and resource disparity as with most international adoption. Additionally, he is aware that Honduras bans homosexual couples from adopting, so he worries about his birth country. He is afraid of traveling there and finding another place to be rejected.

Physical Appearance: His dark skin and straight black hair made blending in with his adoptive family impossible. There were Mexican immigrants in a nearby town, so people often assumed him to be Mexican, which his parents loudly corrected.

Early Experiences and Socialization: Javier was adopted from Honduras into a white family when he was six months old. He grew up in a small town in Ohio without access to a Honduran community, enculturated into primarily white environments. His family encouraged him to be proud of being from Honduras but didn't provide him with resources and opportunities to do that. He didn't know how.

Spirituality: He didn't grow up with any religion but noticed that many Latinos he has met were Catholic. It feels like another piece he is missing.

Socio-Economic Status: His adoptive family was solidly middle class and instilled values around self-sufficiency and independence. He struggles with his tendency to judge the cooperative economics and multi-generational living he observes in some Latino families.

School Experiences: Javier did fine and was popular among his friends. He often used humor to put people at ease and became somewhat of a class clown. Javier did his best to minimize the focus on his race. When choosing a language in high school, he chose French, thinking that Spanish would just "reinforce a stereotype" when he wanted to be known as an individual.

Gender Norms: Growing up in a small town, Javier followed the traditional norms of white masculinity. He knew he was gay since he was eight but witnessed other kids getting bullied and teased for not upholding gender norms. It was another form of masking that he had to master for personal safety.

Relationship Norms: Javier grew up in a two-parent heterosexual household, like most of his friends. However, he hasn't seen any Honduran or Latino men in gay relationships, not in person. And he is often hypersexualized and fetishized by the white men he has dated or slept with.

Cultural Attachment: His mom learned about a cultural immersion camp so that he could make friends with other adoptees during the summers after 4th and 5th grade. However, most of them lived too far away, and they lost regular contact. Otherwise, he has no cultural attachment and has gone to extremes to minimize differences between himself and his white peers.

Political Awareness and Orientation: Javier was raised in a conservative small town and has had challenges resolving the differences between his lived experience and the traditional values he was raised with. He also has some awareness of being perceived as a tragic figure as an adoptee who doesn't have much of his culture. He knows by people's reactions that how he claims or doesn't claim his heritage means something, especially to Latinos.

Other Social Identities: His adoptee identity is held close, as both something that separates him from many peers but unites him with other adoptees. His camp experiences gave him a first taste of belonging and an authentic shared experience.

Javier's Racialized Memory:

> *At age 5 or 6, on a family vacation to Florida, his family took the kids to the playground to play. He kept noticing a little girl whose skin and hair looked similar to his own. He shyly approached her to say hi, but she responded in a language he didn't understand. Her family was nearby and also began speaking to him in Spanish. They looked at him so confused, and Javi felt confused,*

too. When his mom noticed what was happening, she came over with her too-big smile and ushered him away politely, explaining, "They don't speak English. It'll be too hard to play with her. Go over and play with your brother." He felt a deep, indescribable disappointment and sadness. Though he understood his mother's words and framing as the problem being that the other family didn't speak English, he also couldn't help thinking something was wrong with him.

<u>Javier and Systems of Oppression:</u> Javier feels the most judgment and oppression in appearance-based racism and homophobia. And though he leans more into his gay identity as he moves into adulthood, there is an unspoken knowing that his sexuality can never be separated from his race. Javier knows he is attractive, intelligent, and kind - a good catch! But the racism within the gay communities he participates in is palpable. He can find white men who want to have sex with him but few that want an authentic, public relationship with him. With Latinos and other men of color, he feels he is missing a crucial cultural identity piece. Where connection seem easy for them, he feels like he's screaming inside a glass box.

<u>Javier's Compassionate, Contextualized Narrative:</u>

I'm a senior in college, and I've decided to stay in California after graduation. I know that my parents did the best they could with what they knew; they're kind people, and we love each other a lot. And they also didn't do a good enough job of making sure I had more access to my birth culture.

For a long time, I blamed myself, thinking there was something wrong with me for not having more Latinx friends, like I wasn't trying hard enough. But I've learned to have compassion for myself and my family. We didn't know what we didn't know. It's not my fault that I didn't grow up knowing how to be Latino. As an adult, I can find new people and make new choices.

I've had to accept and learn to forgive myself for my whiteness. I'll never be white, but I understand there are things I benefit from in my proximity to whiteness. And what else was I supposed to do as a kid? Reject the white kids and wait for the other Latinos who weren't coming or were very different from me? When I was little, I just wanted to belong somehow. So as much as it stings, I admit that I downplayed my race and made myself as white as possible so I could have friends. I didn't know how much hurt that would cause me as a kid. I was doing the best I could.

I still feel ashamed of my proximity to whiteness and my comfort and ease in navigating white spaces. But that's part of why I'm choosing to stay in California. I notice that there are lots of different types of Latinos, different generations, different styles. I'm starting to make friends with lots of different people, especially other BIPOC who I can talk to about my experiences and feel understood. I know I'm more likely to find more people like me here, and I'm hoping I can build some meaningful connections.

I'm taking Spanish classes now and considering going to an immersive Spanish language experience to help with my fluency. Maybe as I get more comfortable, I'll think again about visiting Honduras. It still feels tender, so I don't want to get ahead of myself. Baby steps.

I am curious about what it means to be a gay Latinx person. White spaces have been more comfortable so far, but I know there must be more places to find different kinds of guys interested in a real relationship with me. I've seen a couple of dance clubs I want to try, but I'd like to have regular activities, too. I heard about Latine Pride in San Diego and am considering attending next year.

In general, my four years out here have shown me that there are other possibilities. I'm making friends with different kinds of people. I realize that while I didn't have a choice growing up, now I can make my own decisions and put myself in situations where I have more in common with people like me, more of a chance to connect. Parts of me are still scared that I might never feel whole or find people I belong to. But I know I can try, and I intend to do that.

REFLECTION SIX:

MY COMPASSIONATE, CONTEXTUALIZED NARRATIVE

Take a moment to review Reflections 1-5, considering your contexts and life experiences.

Now, write a compassionate narrative of your upbringing and socialization that acknowledges all the contexts in which you learned to navigate life in your early years.

When finished, ask with gentle curiosity: What did I learn to do to meet my basic emotional needs of safety, significance, and belonging? Who did I become in order to survive?

Forgive yourself.

Or intend to start forgiving yourself. You weren't intentionally trying to do anything wrong; you developed survival skills. People tend to do what works until it doesn't work anymore. Self-forgiveness can be hard work. Therapy can be a good support in this process.

CHANGING YOUR MIND: SHIFTING BELIEFS AND REINFORCING THE NEW YOU

In Reflection One, you identified some thoughts, feelings, and behaviors that described your perspectives about your racial identity. I'm guessing you might feel differently about them now and may not want to carry those into the future.

How do you imagine a future you've never seen? When I introduced the following meditation to my mixed therapists' group, one of my peers said that trying to conceive a new future is in the lineage of Black speculative fiction. What a beautiful way to look at this work! I look forward to speculating and building worlds together.

I believe that people can step out from underneath systems of oppression and mistaken beliefs by:

- Acknowledging what they were taught or unconsciously believe,

- Getting clear about how these beliefs have hurt self and our community, and

- Being willing to examine and change our conscious and subconscious beliefs.

Courage and humility are required.

When you step out from underneath these systems and mistaken beliefs and instead seek true freedom and empowerment, who are you?

Meditation

If you prefer an audio recording, I have a blog post at http://www.neitherboth.com/post/if-it-s-not-yours-give-it-back

Take a few moments to get comfortable and relaxed.

Breathe in clarity, peace, and rejuvenation.

Breathe out the old, the stale, what no longer serves you.

Cleanse and clear.

You are whole.

There is a pure version of you, untainted by lies, a clean slate.

This version is still you. Feel the essence of this you.

This version will help you clarify what's original to you.

You remain as you originally came to be.

All mistakes can be corrected. All foreign objects can be removed.

Sit with this essence of the pure, original you.

Let this version, this essence, imprint on you with a sign, a signal.

Whatever comes to mind is exactly right.

Make an agreement to be mindful of this sign, this signal.

Notice this sign or signal whenever your true essence wants to pull you back to the truth of who you really are, to the original you.

Notice in front of you an organizational system. It could be a file cabinet, a computer, a series of containers, or piles. You are in control of maintaining this system, and you can rearrange it, you can remove items, you can add

new wisdom, and you can clean and dust some of your items. It is within your power, and it is your responsibility to maintain this organizational system.

Now, allow a memory to emerge that made you aware of how racism has negatively impacted your life and sense of self. Whatever comes to mind is the right thing for today. Notice how this memory impacted your senses - what you saw, heard, smelled, tasted, touched. Notice the thoughts and feelings. Try to get a sense of the conflict and what you believe.

Again, ground into the pure essence of who you are, of who you remain.

Hold this memory in front of your organizational system.

Guided by your purest essence, observe the memory begin to separate into what is original to you in contrast to what was taught to you, projected onto you, and affirmed by outside systems. Allow the pieces to shift apart. File or place these pieces in the appropriate categories.

Observe the categories from yourself as you originally came to be.

Consider again the content of this memory. Remember what it previously caused you to believe. From your true essence, what would you rather believe instead? About yourself? About life? About the world? About race? You may need to continue thinking about this, but whatever comes up now is exactly right.

Thank your purest self, and again remember your sign or signal. Know that you can return to this place whenever you feel the discomfort of a belief that is not original to you. You have the power and the responsibility to correct the beliefs that no longer serve you.

Begin your transition back to the present moment. Become aware of the sounds in your space. Wiggle your fingers and toes. And when you're ready, open your eyes.

An Invitation

I invite you to do something useful with those negative narratives about yourself if you want to be transformed and grow into your more authentic self.

Give people and systems back the trash ideas that were never yours. Use the powers you've had to develop to hold the complexity and multiple truths of your mixedness. Embrace the creativity you had to develop to get your needs met by adapting to different environments.

There is something particular about holding complexity and contradiction and not fitting into boxes... developmentally, it does something to the brain that is useful in creating our speculative fiction. Your imagination is a powerful tool. It helps you create a world you haven't yet experienced.

I also want to offer that your brain is elastic, not static. Our brains have many well-worn pathways created by long-held beliefs, programming, and conditioning around our identities. I have a video about that here: https://www.neitherboth.com/post/changing-your-mind Creating a new pathway for a new belief takes intention and consistency. It will be normal for you to fall back into old, well-worn pathways. Commit to re-paving the new path each time you realize you've wandered off.

Change is a process. It's about identifying what you want to change, realistically looking at your readiness for change, using generous repetition and affirmation, and finding language that feels true to you. This exploration is where we will focus for the rest of this workbook.

REFLECTION SEVEN:

HOW I'D RATHER THINK, FEEL, AND BEHAVE

Returning to your list from Reflection One, rewrite the statements in the way you would articulate them from a more healed and empowered place. This is called a *reframe*.

For example, if Javier believes, "I'm an imposter," his reframe could be, "I am authentic. I may not have grown up with Honduran people, but today I am a Honduran American who is learning more about my birth culture."

Language is an essential tool for change. Saying what you want with positive, hopeful language leads you toward a more empowered future. How would you reframe the following statements? Remember to include any phrases you added in Reflection One.

Common Thoughts:

- I'm not _____ enough

- I don't have a right to speak up/show up in spaces

- I can never show up as my whole self

- I don't belong here/anywhere

- I'm not living up to how other people expect me to be based on how I look

- I don't know how to release this discomfort/pain about my race

63

Common Feelings:

- I feel perpetually uncomfortable, like an imposter

- I feel isolated, anxious, fearful, ashamed, sad, uncomfortable, lonely

- I feel guilty about my privilege even though I'm a POC

Common Behaviors:

- Becoming a chameleon

- Becoming invisible, hiding, and making myself small in public spaces

- Emphasizing other identities over my race

- Being awkward and inauthentic

How true do these reframes feel on a scale of 0-10, where 0 is not true at all, and ten is without a doubt? Write a number next to your reframes.

Ignite your creativity: What are some next small steps to get you closer to a 10?

STAGES OF CHANGE

G enerally, the *Stages of Change* were developed to understand patterns of addiction and recovery. However, they can be used to look at any life change we want to make. There are generally six stages of change:

- Pre-contemplation (ingrained in the old habit and not thinking about change)

- Contemplation (thinking about changing the old habit)

- Preparation (planning for successful change, considering barriers to change)

- Action (trying out the new habit)

- Maintenance (practicing the new habit regularly)

- Relapse (going back to the old habit)

You can find more information on Stages of Change here: https://www.neitherboth.com/post/stages-of-change-how-ready-are-you

In the context of changing your mind about who you are, knowing your stage of change can illuminate the possible motivations and resistance to thinking about yourself in a new way. And it provides an idea of what support you need to prepare to move forward.

Let's use an example of an old habit of thought, *I don't have a right to speak up/show up in spaces*, and the corresponding thoughts, feelings, or behaviors you might have in each stage. Then I'll show you ways to affirm and inspire forward movement in that stage.

Pre-contemplation: *I know nobody wants to hear from me, so I'm not saying anything.*

What to do: If you're honestly pre-contemplative, there's not much to DO. But I would start by acknowledging that this is your truth based on your life experiences and that your history has made you partial to evidence supporting this. If you're reading this book, you're interested in change. Through your identity exploration, you may have discovered some unquestioned, pre-contemplative beliefs - start by affirming the life experiences that brought you to this belief.

Contemplation: *Can I change my mind? Do I have something to contribute to community spaces I've wanted to be part of but felt excluded from?*

What to do: First of all, it's ok for the answer here to be, "I don't know." It's ok to be afraid of these questions. A rigid idea like "I shouldn't ever be taking up space here" signals wisdom and self-protection. Compassionately reframed: no one silences themselves like this without reason. And so, look at the pros and cons of inserting yourself into a place where you've been programmed to believe you don't belong and are unwelcome. What could happen in the best and worst-case scenarios? Is it possible your self-limiting belief is not entirely true? Or that it's not true anymore? Or that it's not true in every situation? Asking questions with as much open-mindedness and creativity as possible will open up new pathways in your brain. And some of those pathways lead to peace, transformed beliefs, and healing. Be courageous in your exploration.

Preparation: *I understand this is complex, and there will be times when I need to either step up or step back. How can I create a loose plan to decide how I want to show up and how I'll handle challenges?*

What to do: Continue dreaming and imagining how things could go well if you start showing up and speaking up. As you do that, just note the dissent in your brain related to old thoughts and behaviors. Get familiar with the old practiced beliefs that show up and plan to address them. I also want to prepare you that in the moment, you may have a fear response that inhibits your ability to think clearly. That's why it's so important to plan ahead of time.

- Use breathing exercises to calm your nervous system.

- Prepare a set of qualifying questions (In my gut, does this feel like the right time and place? Does this need to be said? By me? Now?).

- Consider starting by saying something brief and more general and observing the reaction. If the response is open or positive, step up - say a little more, add a few details. If the response is negative, congratulate yourself for being courageous enough to take the risk, and then step back.

Action: *I'm showing up more consistently now. I seek places where I'm getting more experienced and comfortable talking about my race with others. I balance social and political risks with courage in settings where I sense I have something valuable to contribute, even if I don't say it to the whole group.*

What to do: In practicing new thoughts and behaviors more, continue noticing how you feel about the change. Follow the good feelings! Understand and expect that there are triggers out in the world. Through continued practice in addressing them, you're beginning to understand your skill and confidence in re-directing yourself, calming your nervous system, committing to the changes you've made, and comforting and caring for yourself when your risk didn't go how you'd hoped. Know that sometimes it's them and not you. Ground into this balance: *Sometimes it's best to allow others to take up space depending on the time and place, and sometimes my voice is a valuable and nuanced contribution to the setting.*

<u>Maintenance</u>: *I don't always think I'm in the right place for my voice to be heard, but I intentionally find places where my voice is welcome and talk through things there regularly (trusted individual friends or groups, in specific hashtags, engaging with certain people on social media).*

What to do: Take the opportunity to celebrate your accomplishments on your own and within trusted, caring, compassionate circles. To have come out of self-imposed exile and to learn and practice showing up in your life is incredible! In this stage, you'll continue monitoring your triggers as they come up and actively reinforce your reframe, now with a few real-life experiences to back up your thoughts and beliefs.

<u>Relapse</u>: *I've become discouraged again because of either real or perceived negative feedback. I'm trying to determine what steps I can take to rebuild my confidence and decrease my anxiety.*

What to do: Remember that this is normal. Relapse is a stage in the change process. If you've gone far back enough in your old thinking, you've landed back on that well-worn path. Time to examine what led you back here. What was happening just before things got bad? Was it a specific experience? A particular person's reaction to you? Being around people who reinforced your old path? Mental or emotional health struggles? Changes in social patterns? Reach out to your supports and resources, and maybe work with a therapist if this connects to any deeper core issues or beliefs. Be curious and compassionate as you allow the answers to come. Be gentle with yourself. You've created a way into a new pattern of living, and I trust that you can find your way back - this time with a new or more profound awareness of your triggers and old beliefs and with the experience of developing a plan to address them.

Again, knowing your stage of change helps you to have realistic expectations. Your brain will reject what you don't believe.

We can be motivated to change our long-held beliefs about who we are and where we belong. Still, if there is resistance to the new belief, we may get into some subconscious self-sabotage or other resistant behaviors. In the next section, we'll build on stages of change with affirmations that will help push us into newer, healthier, more affirming beliefs about who we are.

REFLECTION EIGHT:

STAGES OF CHANGE

What risks have you taken in the past when you were trying to change? What were the outcomes?

Select your favorite reframe from Reflection Seven, the one that makes you feel really good, or at least on your way to optimistic.

- What Stage of Change are you in here?

- Generate some ideas to support yourself through this stage.

Select one of the more challenging or surprising reframes for you:

- What Stage of Change are you in here?

- Generate some ideas to support yourself through this stage.

- If you're not ready for change, why? Identify the barriers you can begin working on.

REPETITION AND AFFIRMATION

———

Beliefs are thoughts you keep thinking, and habits are behaviors you keep doing. You have been trained on how to think and act by systems that repeat and reinforce rules and norms until you uphold them yourself.

Confirmation bias says that people tend to favor information that confirms their existing beliefs. Some of your beliefs around identity are very old and well-practiced, and you've likely collected years of confirmation bias around them since childhood. Changing our minds will require intentional bucking of this system and a willingness to practice new beliefs into existence.

When you decide to change your mind, committing to repetition and affirmations will be a valuable tool to - can I put it bluntly? - brainwash yourself. But you are brainwashing yourself into the beliefs and habits you choose for yourself.

To change your mind, choose an affirmation that feels:

- True to you now, on the way to what you would prefer to believe.

- Structured in alignment with whatever stage of change you're in (which will help them to feel true).

- Present tense and positive.

Affirmations have to feel true for them to have any impact on us. Our brains reject what we perceive as untrue (confirmation bias). We don't jump from one end of a belief system to the opposite.

So, say you're working to transform the belief *I don't belong*. Since you've been practicing that belief for so long, your brain may not recognize the opposite belief, *I belong*, as being true. And because of confirmation bias and the rejection of what doesn't feel authentic, it may not be helpful to use those words as the affirmation to support your healing. You may want to start with something softer, such as, "Maybe I can change my mind about belonging."

Considering alignment with whatever stage of change you're in, an affirmation about belonging could look like this:

Precontemplative (not thinking about change): *Other people in my situation have found a way to belong. But that's them and not me.*

Contemplative (thinking about change): *Maybe this is someone else's idea I've taken on, and maybe there are ways I could belong.*

Preparation (planning for change): *I can move toward a feeling of belonging, and I will start trying.*

Action (trying it out): *I am finding ways to belong.*

Maintenance (practicing regularly): *I have a variety of ways I find belonging with people like me.*

Relapse (backsliding): *I have sometimes felt like I belonged, but I've gotten triggered, and now I'm back into old thought patterns, but I can find my way again.*

And once this initial affirmation you choose starts to feel more authentic than your old belief, shift it again - closer toward your chosen belief. In this way, you're building trust and confidence in your ability to change your mind.

Here are some additional examples of positive, present-tense affirmations:

71

I have the tools to explore my race.

I can make different choices.

I feel empowered to make choices about my identity.

I know who I am.

I feel authentic in the complexity of my experiences.

I can acknowledge both my racial privileges and how I've experienced pain and oppression related to my race.

I am an authentic expression of my life experiences and influences.

REFLECTION NINE:

MY AFFIRMATIONS

Remember that with affirmations, you're looking for statements that feel:

- True to you now, on the way to what you would prefer to believe.

- Structured in alignment with whatever stage of change you're in (which will help them to feel true).

- Present tense and positive.

Choose a belief you would like to transform.

Reframe it into the opposite of this belief.

Does it feel true?

If not, practice writing a related affirmation for each of the stages of change:

- Precontemplative (not thinking about it)

- Contemplative (thinking about it)

- Preparation (getting ready)

- Action (exploring and practicing regularly)

- Maintenance (doin' the damn thing)

- Relapse (uh oh)

Once you've found an affirmation that feels true, affirming of your present moment, and matches your stage of change, decide how you want to keep it at the front of your mind as often as possible. Here are some examples:

- Hang it in a place you look regularly.

- Plan to say it aloud ten times at least three times per day.

- Record a voice note with you repeating your affirmation.

- Find a way to use your senses with this new way of thinking about yourself (supercharge your affirmations with sensory triggers):

○ A strong and pleasant scent, maybe an essential oil.

○ Eat a treat or mint.

○ Look at a favorite relaxing photo.

○ Listen to music you love, bilateral sounds, or meditations with a specific frequency for change or healing.

○ Try butterfly taps (crossing your arms and alternate tapping each arm), go for a walk, or do something physical.

A final note: keep working toward action- and maintenance-based affirmations of where you want to be (how you would rather think, feel, and behave).

FINDING THE WORDS

I remember being around eight years old in the mid-1980s when I heard the term mulatto for the first time. Someone described it as a person who is Black and white. It was a poignant moment for me. Previously when people asked me, "What are you," I knew I was supposed to answer, "My mom's white, and my dad's Black." But this was different. Finally! A word to describe ME!

I later learned it means *mule*, a cross between a horse and a donkey, and that it was offensive.

Rapper Latto's original stage name was Mulatto, which I assume was a tongue-in-cheek way of reclaiming a slur. She changed it after much public backlash and personal reflection because of the harmful connotations.

A single word can inspire many thoughts and feelings and can change over time.

If you haven't seen it before, I invite you to look at Maria P.P. Root's Bill of Rights for People of Mixed Heritage (https://www.apa.org/pubs/videos/4310742-rights.pdf) and Multiracial Oath of Social Responsibility (https://www.apa.org/pubs/videos/4310742-oath.pdf).

Language is important, and I think it's essential for you to find language that feels authentic to who you are and your life experiences. Language can be affirming, triggering, or anything in between. What worked for you as a child may have different connotations now. The language you use about your identity is a very personal choice, and may also have social and political consequences.

Some people use the term *minority*; some now describe Black and brown folks as the *global majority*.

Some people may choose to acknowledge their ethnicity or heritage - for example, using *Asian, Asian-American,* or *of Asian descent* - while others might signal specific countries.

Some people are offended by the term mixed and prefer biracial, multiracial, or just stating their ethnic backgrounds.

Some people with parents of distinct races from each other will use percentages, or half and half. And some people dislike the idea of quantifying a person.

Some people use *race* interchangeably with *culture* or *ethnicity*, and others want to be more specific about what those terms mean.

Some people have other identities that are important and inseparable from their race, so they will always include those as an introduction - for example, "I'm a Dakota two-spirit person."

My point is that language is highly subjective, connotations change, and how you refer to yourself may change over time. And all of this is ok.

Remember Javier, the Honduran adoptee who moved to California? As a kid, his parents taught him to stress that he was American, just like them. But today, that is too small of a term for him. He is experimenting with new words for his identity: *Honduran adoptee, Honduran-American, Latino, Latinx, and Latine.* He's trying things out.

Mixed Asians have talked to me about the complexity of describing their race, which has changed with time and clarity. They might use terms like *mixed, Asian-American, hapa, double, biracial, hafu,* etc. Some of these words are geographically, ethnically, or language bound. Sometimes old words still feel right or reclaimed. Sometimes a word that felt good becomes off-limits over time.

I want you to know:

You can change your descriptions over time, letting your identity language evolve over your lifetime.

You can change your descriptions based on the setting. (Some people identify one way at school, another way with family, a different way in diverse BIPOC spaces, and another way in monoracial spaces within their heritage groups.)

You have a right to have the language you use publicly and the language you use privately. You are allowed to protect what feels vulnerable.

REFLECTION TEN:

CREATING LANGUAGE THAT FEELS AUTHENTIC AND ACCURATE

People use many different words and phrases to describe themselves. Consider what feels authentic, accurate, and empowering for you. And remember that you may use some or all of this in various settings depending on your comfort level. Identity is not either/or; it's many overlapping truths. Check all the boxes that feel good to you.

You might use some broad categories:

• Ethnic heritage - African, Asian, Hispanic, Latinx/o/a/ine, Indigenous, etc.

• Nationality - Acknowledging the specific countries in your heritage.

- Skin Color - Black, brown, etc.

- Percentages, wholes, or something in between - decide if saying some variation of I'm half and half feels suitable for you or if you prefer to be this and this.

- Other important identities - some people have different identities integral to describing themselves.

Brainstorm a list of words, contexts, or phrases that feel good and true about you (but note that these don't have to be "feel-good" words):

Create your first draft of how you would confidently describe your lived experience of identity. Feel free to use words or images - be creative in whatever feels right.

NAVIGATING THE WORLD FROM A HEALED PERSPECTIVE: PRACTICAL APPLICATIONS

———

H opefully, I've reached my goal of giving you the tools to begin exploring your identity and acknowledging the contexts in which you developed. At this point, it should be a bit easier to have a peaceful and confident way to articulate who you are.

Identity development doesn't have a forever stopping point. Even if you've come to a place where you're comfortable, a new activating event may switch things up for you. And sometimes, you simply realize you're not as far along as you want to be.

You may decide you need to learn more about aspects of your identity that you weren't enculturated into as a child. However, I want to give a gentle warning: You may not be able to gain a complete sense of belonging and enculturation when you're learning as an adult. While you may want to explore a single cultural group, consider also other types of mixed people.

Avenues to explore include talking to family, engaging with the community, reading and researching and, locating discussion groups and forums.

Some ways I have pushed my development include the following:

- Pursuing relationships with my Nigerian family

- Researching mixed-race and mixed authors

- Doing my practicum at a Black-focused agency

- Group discussions and organizing with Midwest Mosaic

- Going to therapy and doing trauma work around my identities with skilled trauma therapists.

- Facing, learning about, and processing anti-Blackness based on my childhood experiences. Owning up to that and reframing my childhood experiences was pivotal to developing a healthier Black and mixed identity.

For additional resources on exploring identity, the team at Midwest Mosaic and Within, Between, and Beyond helped create an excellent list found here: https://www.midwestmixed.com/resources

REFLECTION ELEVEN:

WORK IN PROGRESS

Given what you have learned, what aspects of your identity need further development?

What do you still want to learn about yourself?

What needs to be unlearned?

How would you rather think? Feel? Behave?

In what ways can you continue on an intentional growth path?

Return to your list of reframes from Reflection Seven and create an action plan to practice/live each statement in 3 different ways.

FACING IDENTITY CHALLENGES

———

C hoosing how to respond to identity challenges is one of the most multi-layered pieces of this process. Facing challenges to your identity is definitely a "many truths" issue. I have to acknowledge that there are complexities to someone challenging the way you choose to identify. We're thinking about:

● Your choice of language and how comfortable you feel using that language with various audiences.

● The identities of the people asking will likely impact how you respond. An old white dude will elicit a different body response than someone from a group you feel shaky about identifying with and where you may have to assert yourself.

● Is this a person you'll never see again? Do you have time today (the emotional capacity, willingness to do labor) to educate a stranger or acquaintance? Is the context safe enough to do this work? Do you have support?

● And with someone you care about, does your relationship have the foundation to take an emotional risk like this?

● Acknowledging particular fears and triggers may point you in the direction of some of your continued identity work. For example, for a Colombian adoptee, knowing that it stings the worst when it's someone from Colombia lets you know you may need to do more development in that part of your heritage.

- There may be age considerations, safety factors, and ways you are expected to show respect.

Identity triggers run deep, especially if there is related trauma. And when our fear/safety/survival center is triggered, you don't have access to the logical parts of your brain. It's good to have some phrases in your back pocket. And to have ways to calm yourself down.

As I stated at the beginning of the book, racial trauma is real. Trauma is anything that was beyond your ability to cope with at the time that it happened. Experiencing identity challenges from a young age can be traumatic - triggering the fight, flight, freeze, fawn, or fall responses.

If you're feeling triggered during a challenge to your racial identity, notice what comes up in your thoughts, emotions, and body sensations. Again, triggers can your body's invitation to learn skills and heal more. Working with a therapist or googling trauma responses and emotional or nervous system regulation skills may be helpful.

A reminder of the importance of learning to regulate our nervous systems: When we are triggered into survival mode, cortisol and adrenaline flood our brains and bodies, forcing a loss of direct connection to the prefrontal cortex, where we integrate complexity and solve problems. We have to wait for the floods to recede before we regain access to the complex thinking parts of our brains. One of the best ways to do that is grounding back into the present moment through our senses and practicing deep, controlled breathing to bring our heart rates back down.

If you get triggered by racial trauma, give yourself time to calm down. Once you're back in a grounded place, return to your affirmations and the reframing work you've done that felt the most empowering. And remember that these are new ideas about yourself - you will need some practice solidifying new brain pathways. It is unrealistic to expect that your corrected beliefs come naturally and immediately. You will need to be intentional and repetitive, giving them practice in new situations and challenges as they come up.

Responding to identity challenges from your new understanding of yourself may be challenging, but practice will make it easier. You may need to take a break and return to important conversations after you have rebalanced your nervous system.

REFLECTION TWELVE:

RESPONDING TO IDENTITY CHALLENGES AS A SELF-AWARE ADULT

Return to the language you created around your identity in Reflection Ten, and imagine someone challenging how you've described yourself. Write down what you imagine they would say.

From a centered, calm, empowered place, try writing some assertive statements based on your new acceptance and confidence in your contextualized identity.

Repeat these exercises with all the experiences that previously triggered you, now grounded into more confidence and the ability to act with intention.

FINDING YOUR AFFIRMING COMMUNITY

———

F inding individuals and communities who can understand, relate to, and affirm you are essential. Community comes in various ways over various identities and subjects.

Know that the way you identify may change based on context and over the lifetime. It's normal to crave different types of community at different times. Sometimes, finding community with others outside of your specific racialized experience will be supportive.

With experiences of identity, sometimes mixed people find commonality with transracial and transnational adoptees, 1.5, or second-generation children of immigrants, and others navigating multiple identities and worlds. Expand your lens on experiences that connect you.

- Local or online groups

- Social media hashtags

- Conferences

CONCLUSION

Identity development can be challenging, especially if you decide to go deep. I hope that I've provided you with the tools to get started in exploring and affirming an identity that feels authentic to you.

I truly believe that identity work is best done in community. I'll never forget this phrase in Irvin Yalom's book about group therapy - *unique wretchedness*. When people have shame-based parts of their identities and journeys, they tend to keep it to themselves, feeding this idea of a unique wretchedness. When we come together to create safe containers and share in a vulnerable way, we find commonalities in our experiences. We see compassion in the eyes of those who can deeply empathize with what we thought was an individual problem.

You can use this workbook alone or with a therapist. But if you can, find friends who can share this journey with you. I will also be facilitating group work, so follow me on social media or join my mailing list if you want to be notified of those offerings.

A final blessing: May you learn to enjoy the sacred variety of your identity, and your life.

REFERENCES:

Carlson, J., Watts, R.E., & Maniacci, M. (2005). Adlerian Therapy: Theory and Practice. Washington, D.C.: American Psychological Association.

Cross, W. E. (1971). The Negro-to-Black conversion experience. Black World, 20(9), 13-27.

Ferguson, E. D. (2010). Adler's innovative contributions regarding the need to belong. The Journal of Individual Psychology, 66(1), 1-7.

Renn, K. A. (2008). Research on biracial and multiracial identity development: Overview and synthesis. New Directions for Student Services, 123, 13-21.

Wijeyesinghe, C. L. (2001). Racial identity in multiracial people: An alternative Paradigm. In C.L. Wijeyesinghe & B.W. Jackson III (Eds.), New Perspectives on Racial Identity Development: A Theoretical and Practical Anthology. New York, NY: New York University Press.

Yalom, I. D. & Leszcz, M. (2005). The theory and practice of group psychotherapy, 5th ed. Cambridge, MA: Perseus Books Group.

ACKNOWLEDGEMENTS:

You know what they say: It takes a village!

I am lucky to have many beautiful people in my life. They have loved and supported me in healing, making it possible for me to write this book. Thank you to my friends and family.

Thank you to John Reardon, my favorite professor turned reader for my thesis. You were the first person to acknowledge this subject matter as my life's work. Years later, we had a magical chance reunion where you gave me the "push" I needed and some good old-fashioned Adlerian ENCOURAGEMENT to get back to this work. Your care, challenges, and questions helped me create the bones that became this book.

Deep gratitude to Amber Phoenix for coaching me through the drafts and completion of this book, helping me to face my fears and move forward with boldness and confidence. "Right hand in left, say YES!"

I believe in the power of change and evolution. Many healers have held my hand on my path. Thank you to the therapists, spiritual teachers, recovery groups, yogis, animals, dance instructors, dance floors, roller rinks, and inspiring loved ones who have supported my healing and expansion.

In the summer of 2020, I collaborated with Leslie Barlow, Ryan Stopera, and 16 magnificent subjects to create Within, Between, and Beyond (http://www.midwestmixed.com/within-between-beyond). In the direct aftermath of the murder of George Floyd, we completed our interviews, and I got to witness and share in so many complex conversations about race, embedded in real-time by the uprising and pandemic. This project forever imprinted on my humanity, my identity, and my work. Special thanks to Leslie, as a processing partner, and a sister.

Endless gratitude to the brilliant thinker and dreamer Alissa Paris, for creating a space to build sacred community and work through complexity. MidWest Mosaic (Mixed) changed my life, nurtured me, and offered me concrete opportunities to contribute.

I'm so grateful to my readers, Sherry Quan Lee, Maya Mineoi, Leslie Barlow, and Ellen Sweetman, for your supportive and critical feedback.

The Mixed Clinicians Collective (http://www.multiracialmentalhealth.com/mixed-clinicians-collective) was formed at the Critical Mixed Race Studies Conference in 2018 and evolved into a sacred community for me to process, connect, and practice. I am blessed by the monthly meetings and individual connections. Thank you so much for your excitement and support around this offering.

And finally, to my clients, past and present. There aren't enough words in the world to describe the deep connection and mutual learning that form the heart of our therapeutic relationships. I thought it might be too niche to create a practice around mixedness and complex identities. But I built it, and you came. You affirmed my hunches, shined a light on my blind spots, and gave my work beauty and groundedness. This book couldn't have been created without you. Thank you for choosing me.

Don't miss out!

Visit the website below and you can sign up to receive emails whenever Lola Osunkoya publishes a new book. There's no charge and no obligation.

https://books2read.com/r/B-A-KFGAB-RBONC

BOOKS 2 READ

Connecting independent readers to independent writers.

About the Author

Lola Osunkoya is a licensed psychotherapist and owner of the counseling practice, Neither/Both LLC. Lola completed a Master's Degree in Adlerian Counseling and Psychotherapy in 2012, where she wrote a thesis on the identity development of mixed-race people. She has created and facilitated racial identity-based content for therapy clinics, county agencies, high schools, universities, and community organizations. Lola uses writing and multimedia art to explore themes of identity, bringing theoretical concepts about race to mainstream art and conversations. Healing from the damaging impact of racism is a central theme of her work.

Read more at https://www.neitherboth.com/.

www.ingramcontent.com/pod-product-compliance
Lightning Source LLC
LaVergne TN
LVHW040053090426
835513LV00028B/592